Group Gathering Discussion Guide

Who Broke My Church?

A 14-Week Adventure in Kingdom Culture

By

Kent R. Hunter

DEDICATED TO

Frank Grepke

—A church leader with a heart for God and a passion to reach the lost.

CONTENTS

Comments from the Author

Years ago, I pastored two very different churches. The first one was in the inner city of Detroit. Long before I arrived, the neighborhood racially changed over a period of two decades, and the congregation ignored it. Most of the remaining members moved to the suburbs and commuted on Sunday mornings to church. They described their church as located "in the 'old' neighborhood." But it was a "new" neighborhood for me and my wife. We lived in the house owned by the church. It was a "new" neighborhood for our neighbors, too!

So, I inherited a beautiful, block-long building and a group of 100% Anglos in a neighborhood of 95% African Americans. The church had declined by 67% in the previous decade, prior to my arrival. I had just concluded three and a half years of graduate school to earn a Ph.D. Before that, I finished four years of college followed by four years of seminary. I thought I knew *something*!

It wasn't long before I discovered 32 people in the church who were bold enough to try a number of outreach *programs*. Nothing seemed to work. I refused to believe that God didn't want the young families in our community to meet Jesus. I would not accept the idea that whites couldn't reach blacks. The power of God's love has to break down the "walls of separation."

Nothing seemed to work. After 18 months of working hard at it, I drifted into a state of discouragement. With that, God opened me up to learn something different.

One day I received a piece of "junk mail" describing the Doctor of Ministry training for busy pastors. It was organized as two-week sessions, three times a year, for three years. The brochure came from Fuller Theological Seminary in Pasadena, California. What caught my attention was the line that said, "Fuller Seminary trains more missionaries than any school in the world." I thought, "Yeah, I'm in a setting like a missionary." (Actually, every Christian is supposed to be a "missionary." You will learn that later, if you haven't already.)

1

In the context of my two-week visits to Fuller, it occurred to me that if you read how Jesus taught His disciples, He started His parables with the words, "The Kingdom of God is like…."

God led me, and that church in that Detroit, to a miraculous turnaround, reaching our community in ways that worked. *But, what really changed was the culture of our people. We became Kingdom people.*

With Kingdom culture, we began to see an explosion of growth, cross-culturally. In addition, most of those in our church would agree: "This has been the most exciting time in my entire Christian life." Many of them were in their 70s or 80s! This church had become a huge church, rapidly growing, with a Christian school with 250 students and a large staff. People began to ask me to write books and consult churches. I mentored a pastor to take my place.

The second church I pastored was very different. It was a rural church on a blacktopped road in the farming area of northeastern Indiana. Five years before I arrived, they suffered a split. Two dominant families tried to "run" the church. (This is a common scenario in small churches, especially in rural areas.) One of the dominant families left, taking many friends and relatives with them. They started another church about seven miles northwest. Those who were left could not afford a full-time pastor. The church had been without a pastor for a while. The church called me to be their half-time pastor.

I began ministry in this rural church by modeling, teaching, preaching, and developing Kingdom culture. In five years, the church grew five times its size and could afford a full-time pastor. By then, my work as an author, consultant, and discipler of other "Church Doctors" became a full-time job.

* * *

Here's what I've come to learn: *It's not about what you do — it's not another program. It's about who you are, who you become. It is about taking on the culture of Jesus, Kingdom culture.* This is how Jesus did it, launching the greatest movement in the history of this planet. Jesus embedded His culture in a few disciples over a three-year period. You can do this, too!

My prayer for you is this: Far beyond being a group *study* (which this is not!), I pray the power of the Holy Spirit will renew *you*. The Apostle Paul wrote about this to the church at Rome: "Do not be conformed to this world, but let God transform you with a complete renewal of the mind" (Romans 12:2).

Don't be offended by this, but most churches have drifted from God's Kingdom culture to some extent. Kingdom culture has five parts: (1) Values — what you consider to be important; (2) Beliefs — what you understand as truth; (3) Attitudes — your posture toward God; (4) Priorities — what you will always do first; and (5) Worldviews — how you understand the Kingdom of God and the way it works.

Most churches have drifted from this culture. Not on purpose — it just happens. While churches fixate on programs and wear people out, Jesus focused on His disciples and built them up. He focused on Kingdom principles. Principles shape everything you do — who you are, 24/7. You don't "attend church." You *are* church. You gather for worship, and that's great. However, the church becomes a destination. For Christians, the real destination is the world.

This is my prayer for you, and everyone in your group, and everyone in your church, and every church, everywhere: that God would lead you to offload worldly ways and reestablish Kingdom culture. Then Jesus will use you to change our world, one person at a time.

Jesus often spoke about seeds, harvest, and fruit. This is the way Jesus' Kingdom grows: organically — like planting a garden. This growth requires atmosphere: sunshine and rain. The atmosphere of your church is important. That atmosphere is Kingdom culture.

Jesus came into this world at a time when Israel was occupied by a foreign army — Rome. How would you feel if a foreign government ruled your land? What if, since you were a child, all you ever heard was, "This land is the land that God has promised to you"? How would you like it if a foreign army moved in and taxed you? How would you feel about your hard-earned cash being sent to a foreign emperor to build monuments and pay armies? You see, Jesus arrived at a season of major discontent among God's people. They felt hopeless!

Today, *discontent* in our world is high. People on drugs, suicides, fear of terrorists, corruption, shootings, moral decay — must I go on? Meanwhile, among God's people, something else is occurring: *holy discontent*. You likely have holy discontent — whether you know it or not. You are about to find out! Holy discontent comes from the Holy Spirit. Holy discontent may be why you are reading *Who Broke My Church?*

Do you want a better world? Do you want greater harmony? Do you want your children, your grandchildren, to live in a world much improved? Do you want to be part of the solution? Do you want your church to have greater impact? All this begins with Jesus, the Prince of Peace. It also begins with you.

Don't read *Who Broke My Church?* like an academic exercise. Soak this journey in prayer. Ask God to shape you and others in your church. As the Lord leads you, consider bringing the *Healthy Churches Thrive!* movement into your church. (For more information see www.churchdoctor.org.)

God is on the move! Pray for others. Invite them to experience *Who Broke My Church? 7 Proven Strategies for Renewal and Revival.* You can't make God bring revival. Neither can I. But most often, if people are receptive, He will bring revival to this broken world. Jesus died so people can live. Enjoy your greatest adventure!

7 Proven Strategies for Renewal and Revival

Group Gathering Discussion Guide

Week 1: Launch Prep

Assignment before you meet for Week #1:
  (1) Read the following items from the *Leader's Guide* on pages 92-107 of this Guide: The Use of Different Words; What is the Goal?; Why is All This So Different?; and What is the Structure of These Group Gatherings?
  (2) Read the introduction to *Who Broke My Church?* (Pages xxiii-xxiv)
  (3) Focus on the book's entire title: *Who Broke My Church? 7 Proven Strategies for Renewal and Revival*

Week #1 Discussion Points

1. Let's start with the title:

   — Who breaks any church?

   — Who is asking that question today?

   — Who *should* be asking that question today?

Discussion Takeaways: _____

_____

_____

_____

2. What about the subtitle?

> — How can you "prove" anything about faith?
>
> — How do you measure faith, which is hidden in the heart?
>
> — When you think about your church, how often are you focused on "strategies?"
>
> — When you go to a store (or purchase online), you may make a shopping list first. That's a strategy! Was Jesus strategic? Is your church?

Discussion Takeaways: _____

_____

_____

_____

3. The subtitle uses the word "renewal."

> — What does that mean for a church?
>
> — What does it mean for you?
>
> — People "restore" old cars, furniture, all kinds of stuff. Is it proper to "restore" or "renew" something holy like your church?

Discussion Takeaways: _____

_____

_____

_____

4. What about that word "revival?"

  — Do you think that means this book will recommend tent meetings with yelling preachers and screaming people? What does it mean to "revive?"

  — Can the people at a church make revival occur? Or is that only God's business?

  — Can church people roadblock revival?

  — In what way do *you* do that? Are you insulted I would even ask?

Discussion Takeaways: _____

_____

_____

_____

5. You read the Introduction to the book before coming together.

  — It talks about an "awakening" — a wake-up call. Do you need that? Does your church?

  — Do you see signs — any signs —your church is "sleeping" as the world goes by? If so, what are those signs?

  — The introduction talks about a movement in England. Did you know about that? Would you like to see it with me? (We take a group every year — 10-12 days and you'll never be the same.)

  — Do you think a movement is beginning here?

  — If you go to the website (www.churchdoctor.org), you can see "Signs of Revival" we have documented.

  — What signs do you see? Any?

Discussion Takeaways: _____

_____

_____

_____

6. Do any of those signs sound familiar?

　　　— Did you see them before? If not, why not?

　　　— Or did you see them but not see them — as signs of revival?

　　　— Are you even looking?

Discussion Takeaways: _____

_____

_____

_____

7. The introduction mentions seven "ceilings" that hinder God's work. They exist in churches.

　　　— If Christ is the Head of His Body, the church, how can damaging ceilings hold the work of Christ back?

　　　— Isn't He all-powerful? So, what's the issue?

　　　— What do you think this "Kingdom culture drift" is all about? Can you name some observable symptoms, tangible results of drift?

Discussion Takeaways: _____

_____

_____

8. It says, in the Introduction, "Kingdom culture is spiritual DNA."

   — People didn't even know about DNA in the Bible. So, what's the point? Does it really exist?

   — If the Bible doesn't use "DNA," what does it say that might relate to what we call DNA today?

Discussion Takeaways: _____

_____

_____

_____

9. The Introduction says God can transform the church.

   — How much would you like to see that?

   — What are you willing to sacrifice to experience transformation? A little? Somewhat? A lot? Be honest, because, as you continue through this book, you're going to find out — and so will everyone else!

   — The Introduction says this is no quick fix. What is your reaction when you take your car in and the mechanic says, "This is not going to be a quick fix"? Fill in the blank, what would you say? "Oh _____!" (Remember you're among other Christians!)

   — The Introduction says, "making disciples is what Jesus commissioned us to do." Does "us" mean you and me, or just pastors and those "crazy" people who like to be on the Evangelism Committee?

   — Be honest, do you even know how, really, to "make a disciple?"

Discussion Takeaways: _____

_____

_____

_____

10. What do you think about this "holy discontent?" Does it sound like an oxymoron, like "hot snow" or "short sermon?"

   — We live in a world of hot showers. Our cars have air conditioning for heat and butt warmers for cold. How can discontent be *holy*? How can anything good come out of *discontent*?

   — What does that imply about the need for CHANGE? (Sorry for using a bad word among church people.)

   — Will you now quit this group and try to get your money back from buying such an awful book?

Discussion Takeaways: _____

_____

_____

_____

7 Proven Strategies for Renewal and Revival

Group Gathering Discussion Guide

Week 2: Chapter One: The Gift of Holy Discontent

1. Can you believe it? A whole chapter for Christians about discontent. And it's called a *gift*!

   — Do you know why an author of such a serious book would attempt silly humor and waste your time? Is it to assess your attitude? Did you know what the Old Testament prophetess Mary Poppins said about humor? She said, "A spoonful of sugar makes the medicine go down." You see, I am a Church Doctor, and I know my stuff!

   — Acts 17:1 is quoted at the start of this chapter. Why? Notice what it says about the Berean Jews: They were of "noble character." What does that mean to you? Does your society, and others, demonstrate tons of "noble character?" How is it that "noble character" connected to the fact that they "examined the Scriptures every day to see if what Paul said was true"?

— Do you have that "noble character," or are you going to disrupt this discussion with your personal opinions? Will you be gracious enough to test EVERYTHING in this book from the position of "noble character?" Do you agree with me: "The Bible is the only playbook we have"?

Discussion Takeaways: _____

_____

_____

_____

2. On the front page of Chapter One, it says, "*You will never do what God wants you to do unless you become who God wants you to be.*"

— Do you buy into that? How much? 100%, 50%, 10%? Really, how much?

— How important is that? God is God. It's His church. Can't He overrule people at will?

— Why would God? Why won't God? Isn't that a lot of pressure on people who are "only human?"

— Did Jesus ever say something like, "With people, not so much is possible, but with God all things are possible"? How does that figure into this discussion?

— Why would Jesus, who is God also, use people to run the church? We have a reputation as "goof-ups." Since God knows everything, should we forgive Him for this one, huge mistake? Why use people like you — and me?

Discussion Takeaways: _____

_____

_____

_____

3. This chapter talks about spiritual atmosphere.

— Wherever your group is meeting right now, what would happen if the atmosphere changed a little? What if it got really hot — 100 degrees Fahrenheit? What if it got really cold — 5 degrees Fahrenheit? What if the electricity went out and it was pitch dark? What if the oxygen content of the air dropped 90%? How important is atmosphere?

— Atmosphere is used as a metaphor for Kingdom culture. How important is Kingdom culture for you? If you rated yourself on a scale from 0 to 100 on Kingdom culture, what number would you pick? No false humility here — there is no -10 on a scale beginning at zero! Beware of rating yourself at 120, too! You'll just signal to the group that you need spiritual counseling. Be honest!

— How would you rate your church, 0-100? How would Jesus rate your church?

— The purpose of this reflective exercise is not to bring on depression. The purpose is this: could you — your church — grow in Kingdom culture? Would a better atmosphere produce more fruit?

— This book is my gift to you as spiritual fertilizer for fruitful results. (No fertilizer jokes, please! I have enough critics!)

— This is serious: How much would you like to see your church produce more eternal fruit for God's Kingdom?

Discussion Takeaways: _____

_____

_____

_____

4. The graph in this chapter on page 3 is about age distribution. It is actually a compilation of hundreds of churches we have diagnosed as part of an onsite consultation. A picture (even a graph) is worth a thousand words!

— What does it say about the state of the church?

— What does it say about the future of the church?

— What does it say about the ability of the church to reach younger generations?

— What does it say about the church's effectiveness to keep those young people after high school? After college? When they have young kids?

Discussion Takeaways: _____

_____

_____

_____

5. This chapter says, "Jesus did not build Kingdom atmosphere using a ten-week Bible study." Before you say it, that's NOT why I made this group gathering 14 weeks long! I will tell you this, to think about. During our years of research, we developed a Kingdom-culture-building movement for local churches. It's called *Healthy Churches Thrive!* It started at 12 months. We weren't satisfied with the fruit — results. We went to 18 months, then two years, and finally, three years. It's embarrassing, because when we found the best results work at three years, someone said, "Yeah, Jesus spent about three years with His disciples!" This effort, which is three years long, is the *Healthy Churches Thrive!* Spiritual Movement. You'll hear more about it later. It's <u>not a program</u>. It's a spiritual movement.

— What do you think? Would you offload a good portion of the busyness that wears out people in your church and redirect your focus on doing what Jesus did — for three years?

— Do you have the faith to believe that growing people will, in time, grow the church, like nothing you've ever seen?

— Looking at the age distribution on page 3 is a hard picture to see. If it hurts you, that's okay. It has hurt me, terribly, for 35 years.

— This chapter talks about pruning: John 15. This is counterintuitive, but we all know it's true. Cutting back produces more fruit. Less is more! It's a miracle! What do you think?

What would you do about it — really? Would you cut back all the activities so God could produce more fruit?

Discussion Takeaways: _____

_____

_____

_____

6. This chapter is a hard swallow for many of us. It focuses on less doing, with more emphasis on becoming. That's a hard sell in today's world.

— What does it mean to you that Jesus commanded His disciples to make disciples? What does that mean?

— What does it mean that Jesus never told the disciples to grow the church? In fact, He said, "I (Jesus) will build my church." What does that mean to you?

Discussion Takeaways: _____

_____

_____

_____

7. There's a whole section on "Recapturing Kingdom" in this chapter (page 7). But we don't live in Kingdoms. Or do we, as churches?

— If Jesus is our King, our citizenship is beyond our national identity. It is in the Kingdom of God.

— How often do you face the realities of this world — the good, bad, and the ugly — from a *Kingdom* perspective rather than just a *national* perspective?

— What is the difference between the culture of our nation and the culture of our Kingdom?

— Do you ever get the two confused when discussing the issues about your church? Can you give examples, without naming people?

Discussion Takeaways: _____

_____

_____

_____

8. Time to discuss (just a little) the pink elephant in the room that nobody wants to talk about. Change. This first chapter has a subtitle "Time to Change" (page 9). That's at the beginning of the book so some people won't have to "waste their time reading the rest of this trash." But it is not trash for people who love God and love their church! It is a big issue, and you can't ignore it. Change! You can't ignore it!

— For now, let's just focus on this: How open are you to *meaningful* change?

— Be honest, what in your church might need to change because it distracts from your primary purpose, your mission?

— What do you hold onto as "sacred," but it really isn't? (Speak out, but also be receptive to comments made by others.)

Discussion Takeaways: _____

_____

_____

_____

My Personal Plan for Spiritual Growth

What is God saying to you about re-ordering your priorities?

_____

_____

_____

What is God saying to you about spending more time in personal Bible study?

_____

_____

_____

What is God saying to you about being more committed in prayer?

_____

_____

_____

What is God saying to you about asking Him to give you an open mind and heart?

_____

_____

_____

Make a plan:

_____

_____

_____

7 Proven Strategies for Renewal and Revival

Group Gathering Discussion Guide

Week 3: Chapter Two: Health Wins

1. This chapter begins with references to the revival we have seen during our years of training pastors on six continents.

    — There hasn't been a real revival in the U.S. or Canada for longer than your lifetime. England has one, right now. (That's why we take people there every year.)

    — Have you ever witnessed a revival firsthand, perhaps in South America, Africa, or even the "underground" church in China? If so, share your unforgettable experience with the rest of the group. (For the rest of you, you need to know it can't really be explained. You have to be there! You have to *experience* it!)

— How would you feel if your church — and others — were growing so fast you could never explain it?

— There is abundant evidence that God may bring revival to other countries as well. What can you do to "prepare the way of the Lord"? What can your church do?

— What *will* you do?

Discussion Takeaways: _____

_____

_____

_____

2. What do you think about God watching?

— Are you a God watcher, always looking at current events to see where God is preparing ground, planting seeds, or even pruning for more fruit?

— How much "God watching" do you look for in your own life? Let's say you lose your job. Are you tempted to cuss out God (even quietly in the recess of your mind)? Or complain? Or worry?

— Or, do you say, "I wonder what God will do with this?"

— If your church is declining, have you "God watched" the subject? Is God sending a message?

— In declining churches, sometimes people blame the society, rock music, TV, even God. What about looking into the mirror? Discuss: What are **you** doing, or not doing, that unintentionally leads to the demise of God's precious organism, your church?

Discussion Takeaways: _____

_____

_____

_____

3. There is a challenging statement in Chapter Two: *"Increased mission and ministry results are not attached to a program. Results are tied to individual spiritual growth of Christians in the church."*

    — This is a hard sell. Everyone loves quick-fix programs. OK — you be the consultant. First, clarify: What is the primary purpose of your church? Why did Jesus die on the cross? Why did He come to this earth? Can you use His own words to make your case?

    — How is your church doing at that? What grade would you give it? Would you have to grade on a curve to avoid spiritual depression?

    — "It's not programs, it's the *individual spiritual growth of Christians in the church.*" How does that make you *feel*?

    — What is God saying to you? And what are you going to do about it?

Discussion Takeaways: _____

_____

_____

_____

4. What is your favorite "God story" (parable) told by Jesus? You've heard these stories for as long as you've been a Christian.

— Go ahead: Share your favorite "God story." Why is it your favorite?

— The parables of Jesus start with, "The Kingdom of God is like...." Or, "The Kingdom of Heaven is like...." (They both mean the same thing.) Have you ever thought about it this way? "If I'm your King, and you belong to me, live like this...." How, personally, do you hear those stories? Do you hear them like they are telling you what Kingdom culture is like?

— On a scale from 1-10 (10 being great), how closely does your life match up with Jesus' God story parables?

Discussion Takeaways: _____

_____

_____

_____

5. How much is Kingdom culture the focus of your church?

    — As you hear, read, and study these parables, *how much are **you** focused on Kingdom culture?* You, personally? What would you say?

    — Since Scripture describes the church as the Body of Christ, how often do you get a checkup? (Smart people get a regular "physical" from an expert. Smart church people get a regular "spiritual" from an expert.)

    — How often, as Christ's Body, do you "exercise" ministry?

    — When children become adults, they usually quit growing taller. Sometimes they begin growing wider, especially in some unmentionable areas. Collectively, as a church, how mature are you? And what shape are you in?

    — Are you watching what you eat? Jesus said, "My **food** is to do the will of the One who sent me." (It means, "I do what God wants.") Does that describe you? Your church?

Discussion Takeaways: _____

_____

_____

_____

6. In this chapter, the book begins to discuss Christianity as a movement, not just as a set of beliefs.

    — Movements move. If I lived in your community, would I describe your church as a movement? Or a building? Or an organization?

    — Is your church outreach fixated on bringing someone to church, to the building, the organization? Or is it a holy infectious center?

    — How do you understand what that means?

    — Are you contagious? Will people outside the church catch Jesus from you? Do you know many non-Christians at work, where you shop, or where you go (or went) to school who caught the overwhelming love of Jesus from you?

    Discussion Takeaways: _____

    _____

    _____

    _____

7. This chapter ends with a daunting question: "As a Christian, what is your vision?"

    — Are you praying for a move of God? Since when? Every day? All the time?

    — Do you really believe that your church can reach your community?

    — Do you have a Kingdom-sized vision? Do your leaders?

— How hungry are you for Kingdom culture? (I'm starving! It's why I wrote the book and this Group Gathering Discussion Guide. Can I ask you for a date to join me at the heavenly banquet? Is the date soon, or will you put it off?)

Discussion Takeaways: _____

_____

_____

_____

7 Proven Strategies for Renewal and Revival

Group Gathering Discussion Guide

Week 4: Chapter Three: Outreach - An Inside Job

1. This chapter begins with a quote by Darrow Miller, one of my favorite authors on worldviews. This quote is powerful! "If the church does not disciple the nation, the nation will disciple the church."

    — Darrow Miller just described the U.S. Maybe other countries, as well. Jesus said, "You reap what you sow." While the church has been sleeping, sowing little, much of the field has become weeds, and we are paying for it dearly. (You should hear me when I'm really negative!)

    — Do you agree? Or disagree? Either way, you're right: It's a mixed bag. How would you explain it?

— But there is hope around the corner. In this chapter, I share the spiritual cycle, as we understand it (page 35). Where do you think your country is right now? Faithfulness? Drift? Ignored prophets? Civilization deteriorates? Hopelessness? Receptivity? Repentance? Share where you think the nation lands, overall. Explain why you picked your choice.

Discussion Takeaways: _____

_____

_____

_____

2. If you read the chapter and came prepared, you already know that our research shows, at least in the U.S., we are in the stage of hopelessness. I believe this is an important time for the church. You snooze, you lose! A short note about that: When this book went on sale, the first printing was sold out in two days! At first, I was angry that our truly great publisher messed up and should have printed a gazillion copies. Then one of my colleagues hit me up against the side of my head (verbally, not physically) and told me one of *my* favorite lines. "You're looking at the glass half empty," she said. My point: Christians are not snoozing. They are hungry for help! God is on the move!

— What are the signs of hopelessness you see in the society?

— How does this reshape your strategies?

— How does this fire your enthusiasm?

— How does this impact the way you do church? (That's a big one!)

Discussion Takeaways: _____

_____

_____

_____

3. Hope in Christ fuels the ability to retool for effectiveness in your church.

— How many people in your church would have a clue as to how hopeless unbelievers feel?

— How receptive are people to Christ — if reached in the right way?

— How uncertain are you about the best ways to reach them?

— Do those in your church recognize the power of Kingdom culture?

Discussion Takeaways: _____

_____

_____

_____

4. This chapter circles back to change (We know church people can't hear too much about change, too often). Here I shared one of my favorite sayings, from John Maxwell. Change has three parts. You are ready to change:

(1) When you hurt enough, you have to change.

(2) When you learn enough, you want to change.

(3) When you receive enough, you are able to change.

— Discuss these three areas, as they relate to your church: For each one of the three,

       o   Identify examples of evidence in your church.

       o   See if you can come up with a consensus of where you are on the journey for each one as a % of "Yeah, that's us!" (1% = almost not at all and 100% = over the cliff.)

Discussion Takeaways: _____

_____

_____

_____

5. In this chapter, I went a little deeper with the concept of holy discontent as well.

— It says, "People who have holy discontent are seeds for an awakening in your church." Are you one of them? Can you share your discontent, without just sounding like another "church complainer?"

— Have you taken the survey on holy discontent? If you read the chapter, you probably have. Can everyone share if they have been infected by the Holy Spirit with holy discontent? (Remember — this is the work of the Holy Spirit, in God's timing. It literally has

nothing to do with the individual's faith or love for God or the

church.)

Discussion Takeaways: _____

_____

_____

_____

6. Look at the "Stream of Revival" graphic in this chapter (page 46).

— Everyone: Take a stab at where you think your country is right now.

— What is the consensus?

Discussion Takeaways: _____

_____

_____

_____

7. This chapter relates that in every kingdom, country, and nation-state, there were

some cultural norms set up by whomever were the founders and leaders. They

provide cultural values. Throughout history, all these entities constantly drifted

from the culture of the leaders. So, the leader would have special ambassadors, called "apostles," to correct kingdom (or country) cultural drift. These special ambassadors were called "apostles," even before New Testament times.

— This is important for God's Kingdom, because Kingdom drift diminishes Kingdom results. Would you be willing to share with your group a time when you drifted from God's Kingdom culture?

o What pulled you away? What or who did God use to pull you back?

o Did you ever imagine them in the same role as the apostles of ancient history? (I'm not talking about the special Apostles of the New Testament, but the role of apostles, who remind people of cultural values.)

— As a group, discuss *how* your church may have drifted from Kingdom culture.

— Can you pinpoint how that drift, which is natural, first started to occur?

— How many of you really believe return from Kingdom drift could reignite health and outreach growth in your church? (Don't be bashful; be honest. It's OK if you're not convinced — yet.)

— What would it look like in your church to experience renewal? What might be some tangible fruit?

Discussion Takeaways: _____

_____

_____

_____

7 Proven Strategies for Renewal and Revival

Group Gathering Discussion Guide

Week 5: Chapter Four: The Culture of the King

1. This chapter begins by describing Jesus' two missions: #1 to come into this world to pay for the sins of everyone who believes in Him — to take away the punishment we deserve.

    But the world was supposed to continue. So, mission #2 was to set up a Kingdom that would continue to introduce people to this resurrected Savior.

    — How well do *you* "get" the first mission, your personal salvation through the death and resurrection of Jesus? On a scale of 1-10, 10 being "I really get it."

    — How would you rate your level of "get it" about the second mission, your personal role as an ambassador for this King, to grow Kingdom culture in believers who effectively lead new people to a personal relationship with Jesus? Rate yourself on a scale from 1-10.

— How would you rate your *church* on mission #1? (scale from 1-10)

— How would you rate your *church* on mission #2? (scale from 1-10)

— Someone do the math — what is the group average number for mission #1? Mission #2?

Discussion Takeaways: _____

_____

_____

_____

2. Perhaps one of the most challenging issues of Kingdom culture is in this chapter. "How can you be successful (or effective) as defined through the lens of Jesus?" It's not something "normal" to human beings. (I admit, I have to ask God for strength to fight this all the time.) We human beings, those like me, want to go *big* and go *fast*. But, I'm learning from Jesus. In order to launch the greatest movement in world history, He started *small* and went *slow*. WHAT? In a nutshell, this is the approach of discipling.

— Can you trust God to start small and go slow? (Be honest, and you won't be embarrassed by the next question!) Gather the group's thoughts about this.

— You know what Jesus did. He gathered 12. They got most of His attention most of the time. He spent His most important three years with them. It's called discipling. Here's the question: Who have you discipled like this?

— How *many* people have you discipled like this?

— Do you ever catch yourself thinking that others will become Christians if you just fill their heads with the right stuff about Jesus? Or, just get them to plant their rear ends into a seat at worship?

— This chapter says, "The miracle of the movement (of Christianity) is not limited to one big crowd listening to one great speaker. This movement is all about every believer imprinting others, one person at a time." Does your church mirror this? Do you?

Discussion Takeaways: _____

_____

_____

_____

3. Are you involved in some "quick fix" program at your church? Try raising kids that way! Making disciples is like raising children.

— So, how does your church perform? Does your church have "ushers" for worship, or "greeters?" Do they have someone with them, following along, being discipled? Always?

— What about you? Are you involved in any ministry? If so, are you discipling someone in that ministry? Are you raising them like another child of God, discipling them for ministry?

Discussion Takeaways: _____

_____

_____

_____

4. This chapter has one of the most dramatic graphics of the thousands of data profiles we see at Church Doctor Ministries. It is one of our most insightful survey questions, in my perception: "Did You Become a Christian Before You Started Attending This Church or After?" (page 57). It demonstrates how good your church is at reaching people who are non-Christians (the largest group in the U.S. and most countries). Even more, it shows the "trend of effectiveness" over time. The results make me cringe every time I look at it. For example, as America becomes less Christian, the effectiveness to reach them has diminished. WE DON'T KNOW HOW TO REACH THE UNCHURCHED!

— What do you think your church's profile would look like?

— On a scale of 1-10, how well do you feel equipped to reach people far from God?

— How many unchurched people has God used you to bring into the Kingdom of life with Jesus?

Discussion Takeaways: _____

_____

_____

_____

5. There's an old saying, "What gets measured, gets done." So, what does your church measure? Attendance at worship? Financial giving? Baptisms of previously self-declared non-Christians? Does your church measure how many have been discipled for two to three years by a more mature Christian? How many become a discipler to disciple others? Do you measure the number of those who have been discipled for hospital ministry?

— How does what you measure show your priorities as a church?

— What don't you measure that would be the priorities of your King, Jesus, and His Kingdom?

— Honestly, I don't mean to be offensive! These are hard questions to ask, to hear, and to answer. Renewal in the church is challenging! Follow what the Apostle Paul told the Ephesians (Chapter 4),

"Speak the truth in love." I love you and your church. And all this is the truth!

— How do you feel about these issues? Angry? Defensive? Troubled? Challenged? Eager? Excited? Be honest, speak the truth in love about how you feel.

Discussion Takeaways: _____

_____

_____

_____

6. In this chapter, the elements of Kingdom culture are listed in detail: (1) Values, (2) Beliefs, (3) Attitudes, (4) Priorities, and (5) Worldviews (pages 62-64).

— Is this new to you? If so, why, do you think?

— Do you see how this could be helpful Kingdom teaching for you? For your church?

— Can you commit these components and their descriptions to memory?

— Can you make them part of the culture of your church and the One who founded this movement?

Discussion Takeaways: _____

_____

_____

_____

7 Proven Strategies for Renewal and Revival

Group Gathering Discussion Guide

Week 6: Chapter Five: Turn Your Church Right-Side Up
Breakthrough Strategy #1

1. The strategy in this chapter breaks through *The Ceiling of Corporate Confusion* (page 75). Somehow the church has fallen into an identity crisis. Every metaphor in Scripture that refers to the church is a living organism: sheep and shepherd, vine and branches, citizens of the Kingdom, etc.

   In the 36-month Spiritual Movement for congregations called *Healthy Churches Thrive!,* one of the component Bible studies is called *Six Faces of the Christian Church*. It is a fascinating study of all the images in the New Testament that reflect how this divine organism, church, is supposed to run. Why do most churches operate as religious corporations?

— Do you have corporate meetings in your church that operate according to bylaws? Do you have elections? Do you have some board that is considered the decision-making group of the church? Do people cast votes in some way? All of this is a corporate model that does NOT reflect the biblical structure of church: not in spirit or form.

— Do you know all the metaphors used in Scripture to describe this beautiful creation called "church?"

— How did we ever get to be so much like the world?

Discussion Takeaways: _____

_____

_____

_____

2. Most churches are designed functionally, with a top-down structure.

— Did it energize you to read in this chapter?

— Why do you think the church is designed as a flat organization, not a hierarchical organization?

— Does your church reflect an organization or a family?

— In Scripture, *the church is not built* to be political, hierarchical, denominational, or institutional, but relational. How close is your church to that?

— The church operates like your human body; every part is important. What percentage of those in your congregation even know their spiritual gifts?

Discussion Takeaways: _____

_____

_____

_____

3. In this chapter it says, *"The organizational structure of most churches is a major roadblock for thriving Christianity"* (page 78).

— How does that strike you? Radical? Biblical? Surprising?

— How do you think the church became so much like an institution and so unlike a family, or a team, where everyone is a minister, or a pruned vine that produces tons of fruit?

— How do you feel about the disrespect for authority in our country? What about in your church? Do you see this arrogance in the church toward the pastor(s)? Leader(s)? Jesus? The Bible?

— Consumerism is rampant in our country. What about in the church? Do you see it in your congregation? Does it creep into your Christian life?

— What about entitlement mentality? It's a curse in any society. What about in the church? "I'm a church member. I come here once in a while. I put a little money in the offering. I should have a say. I don't

know what the Bible says, but I think...."

Discussion Takeaways: _____

_____

_____

_____

4. What would occur if we became clear about what it means to be in Kingdom

culture? This chapter includes one of my favorite metaphors about how the

Kingdom works: yeast (or leaven). Yeast is (1) practically invisible; (2) takes a

long time to work in dough; (3) changes everything! How cool is that!

When you become a citizen of the Kingdom, you don't get signed up for a bunch

of programs. It's not what you do, but who you are. The word "yeast" in the

Bible refers to "unconscious influence." You act, you influence, *unconsciously*,

not because you are part of a program, but because you are a Kingdom person

— it comes naturally. (Actually, it comes supernaturally!)

— Have you ever heard this before? What does it tell you about how Jesus

intends us to *be* church, not *do* church? What do you think?

— When you *are* church, you don't need a program. Don't you think Jesus

is brilliant?

— Is your church over-programmed?

— What if everyone was properly discipled and everyone would BE church, everywhere, all the time? Would there be any need for programs?

— Do you think, by God's power, people can BE the living, breathing, loving, serving, witnessing church, everywhere they go, through "unconscious influence?" Not by doing, but by being!

— Or was Jesus so unrealistic this could never happen?

Discussion Takeaways: _____

_____

_____

_____

5. This chapter covers the breakthrough insight of low control/high accountability (pages 94-95).

— Is that how you would describe your church?

— Is that how you operate with work associates?

— How would this change your life?

— How would this change your church?

— How would this change your family?

Discussion Takeaways: _____

_____

_____

_____

7 Proven Strategies for Renewal and Revival

Group Gathering Discussion Guide

Week 7: Chapter Six: Turn Your Church Inside Out
Breakthrough Strategy #2

1. The strategy in this chapter breaks through *The Ceiling of Country Club*. This chapter is based on another research question we use in every church we consult (page 96).

   — What would you say is the main purpose of the church? Choose one of the following answers:

   o To teach people how to live the Golden Rule.

   o To be the moral backbone of society.

   o To make disciples.

   o To provide a place of fellowship, to share God's love with one another.

Fifty-seven percent of people across 67 denominations, independents, and non-denominational churches — tens of thousands — of them say the main purpose of the church is "to provide a place of fellowship to share God's love *with one another*." Welcome to the country club church!

— Do you feel insulted to think of a church as a country club? How does Jesus feel?

— What do you think this survey question would show in your church?

— What would you say if you hadn't read about this in the book?

I think Jesus would roll over in His grave to know that more than half of church people would rather have fellowship with each other than make disciples (which got only one-third of the votes, 34%). (Of course, Jesus rose from the grave, so He has no place to roll over. But I bet He weeps!)

— Would you weep at this rejection of the Great Commission by two-thirds of your congregation?

— What does this say about declining churches? (It's not the *whole* issue — BUT REALLY?)

— Are you as thankful as I am that Jesus loves and forgives us?

Discussion Takeaways: _____

_____

_____

_____

2. But there is hope. You saw the graph in this chapter (page 100). In just six months of the *Healthy Churches Thrive!* Spiritual Movement, it jumps to 68% — more than two-thirds! This is the power of nurturing Kingdom culture!

— There is much more to being a healthy, growing church than this. However, wouldn't it be a good start?

— Why do you think such a large percentage of people don't get the purpose of the church? Most church and denominational constitutions have a purpose statement that quotes the Great Commission from Matthew 28:19-20 — "Go make disciples, baptizing and teaching." Why do you think we suffer so much drift concerning our main purpose?

— What if Ford forgot they made cars?

Discussion Takeaways: _____

_____

_____

_____

3. The direction of the Great Commission is described in the very first word: Go!

    — Why do you think we are so hung up on the strategy of inviting someone to church? ("Y'all come.")

    — What would it take to turn your own mind inside out on this one? How about your life?

    — Can you actually reprogram your thinking from "bring a friend to church" to "take church to your friend"? Of course you can! Will you?

    — What would it take to turn this around for your whole church?

    Discussion Takeaways: _____

    _____

    _____

    _____

4. Why would someone ever say, "If you have an unchurched friend who shows a little interest in spiritual matters, don't take your friend to church. Take your friend for coffee" (or breakfast, or fishing — whatever)?

    — Can you understand that people go to church to worship God? Why would a nonbeliever want to go to worship a God he or she doesn't (yet!) believe in?

    — Do you think your whole church could turn inside out? How would that be accomplished, by God's power? Using what strategy?

Discussion Takeaways: _____

_____

_____

_____

5. This chapter says your church building has only two major purposes: worship

    and equipping (Sunday school, Bible classes, etc.)

    — Do you think we might rely too much on church buildings, to the

      extent that we get the idea the church is a destination?

    — Doesn't the Bible say that "God so loved the WORLD…."? Isn't the

      WORLD our destination? Have you always seen it that way?

    — The church is a launchpad for mission and ministry. How can you

      get that embedded in the lives of those in your church, beginning

      with your own worldview?

    Discussion Takeaways: _____

    _____

    _____

    _____

6. This chapter referenced the word "missionary." It does not actually appear in

    Scripture. The word "missionary" comes from the word "send" translated into

    Latin (in the Latin Bible, centuries ago!) "missio," and from that, we ended up with the words "mission" and "missionary." However, it is a good word because it stands for and implies that every Christian is *sent* by God. Therefore, you are a missionary.

— If you ask those in your church, "Who knows a missionary?" you will see a few people raise their hands. A few will tell you about someone they know who went to serve God overseas. Then you can tell everyone to go look into a mirror. Every Christian is a missionary. Every Christian is "sent" by God, to be on His mission, all the time!

— How would that change the self-image of the people in your church?

— How would it change the image of your church?

— How would it change your effectiveness to reach lost people for Jesus?

Discussion Takeaways: _____

_____

_____

_____

7 Proven Strategies for Renewal and Revival

Group Gathering Discussion Guide

Week 8: Chapter Seven: Turn Your Faith into God-Sized Potential Breakthrough Strategy #3

1. The strategy in this chapter breaks through *The Ceiling of Baby Food*. The Apostle Paul wrote to the church at Corinth. In 1 Corinthians 3:1-3, he expressed frustration because of their "spiritual dealings" with each other. That was the symptom. Paul nailed the cause: They were "like infants in relation to Christ, 'nursing at the breast.'" They hadn't matured by feeding on the "meat" of Scripture. They were adults stuck on a spiritual nipple! It's a little gross, but I'm sure Paul got his point across. You may not hear a sermon explaining it so dramatically. But you would, if Paul was your preacher, and I think most Christians need to hear it. However, try preaching that to churches filled with people convinced a 15-minute preaching

message once a week makes them mature enough to handle this complicated world!

— How deep in God's Word are the people in your church?

— How deep in God's Word are you?

— How would you rate your knowledge of Scripture?

Discussion Takeaways: _____

_____

_____

_____

2. As an author of 31 books about Christianity, with a Ph.D. in theology and a D.Min. degree in church growth, what do you think *I think* I know? I work at being in the Bible every day. When I'm not traveling, I'm with my wife in Bible class. And I continue to learn so much — every Sunday. When we consult churches, there are often challenges from certain people in the church. We politely ask them about how they go about learning from Scripture. The truth? Many are biblically illiterate — or know just enough to be dangerous! If churches would give out grades, like schools, many Christians would fail! Here is the point: It's not about how much you know. It's about how much you are learning — all the time.

— What is the culture at your church about Bible study?

— Are leaders chosen from among those who have a lifelong lifestyle of Scripture learning?

— What is the level of biblical ignorance in your church? How many lifelong Christians are still at a third grade level of Bible knowledge? (No, don't even think about telling them they're on the spiritual nipple!)

— How many people do you know who demonstrate by their lifestyles that "a sermon every Sunday" is enough?

— The Scripture is spiritual food. How many people are starving to death, spiritually? Who do you know that could survive on a 15- to 20-minute meal once each week?

— How anemic is your church? You can learn by diagnosing the percentage of those in Bible study (of any kind) as an ongoing lifestyle.

Discussion Takeaways: _____

_____

_____

_____

3. What is the perceived level of biblical authority among those in your church? Many Christians have conveniently disregarded parts of Scripture that seem too

"spooky" or don't fit with cultural norms of our spiritually bankrupt society. This is what I've learned about every revival where I've taught pastors and churches (about 25 different times): Every group of pastors experiencing revival believes this same concept: "The God of the Bible is the God of today. Anything that occurred in the Bible can and does occur today."

— What do you think about that?

— Can you agree with that?

Some will say this is naïve. Others will say this is not sophisticated. Jesus said, "Believe like a little child." You don't have to understand it. It doesn't have to seem like reality to you. That doesn't make it a fairy tale! Don't you know there was a time when people thought that if you sailed far enough, you'd fall off the earth? Yet some went farther, traveled beyond, and discovered a whole lot more!

— What do you believe about the Bible?

— Are you a "sophisticated" believer in this scientific age, so sophisticated that you can't grasp certain issues as real because you haven't experienced them?

— Have you ever considered that you haven't experienced them perhaps because you haven't believed?

— People today have turned it around. The world says, "Seeing is believing." The Bible says, "Believing is seeing." Get it? Where do you place yourself on that one?

— Do you say, "I just can't buy into that?" Of course you can't. Faith comes first. "Faith comes from hearing that which comes from preaching Christ" (Romans 10:17, one of the most sophisticated portions of Scripture). You need faith — to believe at all!

Discussion Takeaways: _____

_____

_____

_____

4. According to the graphic in this chapter (page 122), among all the churches, only 36% of those in worship attend a regularly scheduled Bible class. When a church is involved in the *Healthy Churches Thrive!* Spiritual Movement, it jumps to 51% in six months! Still, that's only half the people. That's one of the reasons the *Healthy Churches Thrive!* spiritual movement doesn't end at six months, but at 36 months!

— How do you think biblical illiteracy cripples the effectiveness of your church?

— What if you looked at a school for your child and discovered only 51% of the teachers were "certified," but they never continued their education? Would you call that school successful? Would you feel comfortable with your child in that school? How do you think God feels about His children?

— How do you think God feels about such low interest in the only manual He's given us?

Discussion Takeaways: _____

_____

_____

_____

5. In our research, it seems that two types of Christians bail from rigorous Bible study: #1 are those who are arrogant and think they know it all, and #2 are those who play the role of false humility, who say "I'm just too busy" — which is a half-truth. If you *are* too busy to learn from God's Word (and that's not just an excuse), you *are* too busy. Your priorities are wrong, *even if your busyness is church-related.*

— Do you have the spiritual *humility* to say, "There is so much of God's wisdom I don't know yet?"

— Do you have the *humility* to confess you are too busy because your priorities are wrong?

— Do you have the *integrity* and *discipline* to make the right choices?

— Do you have the *awareness* to recognize you are robbing yourself and contributing to the death of your church?

— Do you have the *clarity* to understand that, perhaps, you are planting seeds in your children about the low value of God's Word that you will regret for eternity?

— Can you change your lifestyle for six months and learn how much you are missing by not feeding on God's Word? (If you do that, you may never go back to spiritually starving yourself.)

— Does this issue partially explain why so many churches are wasting away like people in a concentration camp? You can help change that! After all, it's the *healthy* churches that thrive!

Discussion Takeaways: _____

_____

_____

_____

7 Proven Strategies for Renewal and Revival

Group Gathering Discussion Guide

Week 9: Chapter Eight: Turn Up Your Fire for Change
Breakthrough Strategy #4

1. The strategy of this chapter breaks through *The Ceiling of History's Mysteries*. It is the dangerous habit of hanging onto styles of *religion* from previous eras. This is about clinging to worn-out vehicles, the *packaging* of the content. It broadcasts the image to unbelievers that God is out of date and irrelevant. It is a huge roadblock to reach new people for Christ. It's a symbol of unconscious selfishness on the part of believers who are called to reach the world. It is focusing on "religion" at the expense of "faith." It was the practice of Pharisees.

— Do you find change difficult? Do you know that's normal?

— Would you change occupations in order to feed your children?

— Would you change your church habits to increase the potential of your children's eternal future?

Discussion Takeaways: _____

_____

_____

_____

2. Continuing on the issue of your children's eternal welfare, millions of Christian parents have been unwilling to give up their version of Christian music and seating arrangements, like pews. They have found the vehicles "comfortable" since their childhood. However, they have inadvertently helped run their children out of the Christian faith.

— Does your church meet in a building that looks like the God you worship is alive and real for people who are now 15-20 years old, carrying an iPad?

— Does your church use the technology used by most of the rest of the world?

— Do you believe the medium (packaging/vehicle) projects a message?

— Would you trade your favorite hymn book for words on a screen?

— Would you trade the organ for a worship team with guitars and drums if it connected to your 19-year-old headed into a secular society or a secular university?

Discussion Takeaways: _____

_____

_____

_____

3. The *substance* of Scripture must never change. Ironically, many of the Christians who have considered it more important to sync up with today's unbiblical culture have, at the same time, clung to the *style*, the packaging of several centuries ago! This is the classic case of focusing on religion and abandoning spiritual faith. This is the tragic mistake the Pharisees made about Jesus.

— Are you clear about the *substance* of your faith, unwilling to depart from it?

— Are you clear about the *style* of your faith which, ever since Jesus walked this earth, has continually changed to fit the intended audience?

— Do you recognize *tradition*? It is the recital of heroes of the faith who trusted God to do what others thought impossible. Read Hebrews 11. It is the *living faith* of the dead.

— Do you recognize *traditionalism*? It is the *dead faith* of the living. Faith in things, styles, habits, buildings, instruments, songs, pews, etc.

Discussion Takeaways: _____

_____

_____

_____

4. Openness to innovation and change is a biblical issue. It is also an issue of mission effectiveness. The passion to reach people for Christ drives Christians to clarify theology objectively from God's point of view. People matter to God. All the tools are simply vehicles for what really matters. If you want to get to town, you can still ride a mule. However, if time and town are really what's important, your automobile may work more effectively for you.

Monitoring the *Healthy Churches Thrive!* Spiritual Movement, our research shows significant change in perspective when the mission of Christ dominates the landscape of your church. The percentage of people who focus on the future rather than the past grows from 37% to 65% in the first six months! (See the graph on page 146.)

— Change is difficult because it is uncomfortable. But God doesn't change. Do you think most church conflict is tied too much to things and not to God?

— Can people in your church live with Jesus' injunction to His followers, when He said "deny yourself"? (Luke 9:23).

— Can people in your church learn from Paul's admonition, "Consider others more important than yourself?" (Philippians 2:3-4).

— Have we drifted to the point where feel-good church is so important that we resist change at the expense of effective mission to the lost?

— Has the self-centeredness of secular society crept into your church — and into your mind, or heart, or both — and crippled God's power in you to reach the unchurched?

— Is this, perhaps, one of the reasons why most churches have almost completely lost a whole generation of young people?

Discussion Takeaways: _____

_____

_____

_____

7 Proven Strategies for Renewal and Revival

Group Gathering Discussion Guide

Week 10: Chapter Nine: Turn Your Strategy into God's Math Breakthrough Strategy #5

1. The strategy in this chapter breaks through *The Ceiling of Addition Addiction*. It's about the reality that most churches and Christians look at Christianity as an institution, a program, and a building instead of a movement. Consequently, we seem stuck on the idea of growth by addition. However, the genius of Jesus' movement is multiplication x multiplication = exponential growth by geometric progression. In other words, we are trapped by mediocre expectations and microscopic vision. This is not a "mathematical program" issue; this is a "faith potential" issue.

   — When you consider your church, in all honesty, do you think you sometimes settle for puny results?

— The Bible says, "All heaven rejoices over one sinner who repents" (Luke 15:7). But Jesus also told His disciples, "The harvest is large…" (Matthew 9:37). In John 15:6, Jesus says, "By this my Father is glorified that you bear *much* fruit and so prove to be my *disciples*" (italics mine).

— What do you think all this means?

Discussion Takeaways: _____

_____

_____

_____

2. Under the subject of "Heavenly Math," this chapter says, "one of the enemy's most sinister tricks is to rob you of God's breakthrough mathematical strategy." The concept of making disciples, who make disciples, who make disciples — is God's strategy of multiplication. It is the genius of movement.

    — Can you share how many people you have discipled (including your kids) who are not only disciples of Jesus, but disciplers for Jesus?

    — Is this a clearly articulated, well-known, clearly understood lifestyle of those in your church? If so, how did that occur? Do you realize how rare (sadly!) that is in churches

— If this multiplication is not part of the culture of your church, why not? Do you disagree with my understanding of movement multiplication? If so, why? If you agree, how will you help change this in your church? In your life?

Discussion Takeaways: _____

_____

_____

_____

3. Many churches are staff-led. At Church Doctor Ministries, we believe God uses leaders to — well, lead. There is a spiritual gift of leadership. Today, many talk about "staff-led" churches. This leadership is great, but for many, it means "the staff does all the ministry."

    — What is it like at your church?

    — In Ephesians 4:11, Paul says that the role of leaders ("staff people") in the church is to "equip God's people for the work of ministry, which results in the growth of the Body of Christ and an atmosphere of God's miraculous love" (verse 16). Do you think this approach would change your church?

    — Can you imagine: (1) if everyone in a church knew their spiritual gifts? (2) if they were discipled to do ministry? (3) if the staff spent most of their time equipping the people for ministry? (4) if, once discipled as disciplers, the people discipled others? Could the people, in their spare time, do more ministry than paid staff, working 50-60 hours a week? This is the genius of Jesus. How do you think we can get back to this?

Discussion Takeaways: _____

_____

_____

_____

4. One of the keys to multiplication is, of course, discipling. This chapter has the four discipleship steps (page 169): #1: I do/you watch; #2: I do/you help; #3: You do/I help; and #4: You do/I watch. You could add two more steps — one at the beginning: "Come, follow me" (the invitation to be discipled). The second would be at the end: "Go and do likewise" (become a discipler).

— Do you think discipling is as difficult as physics? Of course not! My children learned this at age 10! Did yours? Did you?

— Here's a shocker: I didn't learn this at age 10 or even at the seminary! I thought it was just the seminary I attended. After working with thousands of pastors from nearly a hundred different backgrounds, I've learned most pastors NEVER learned this! Is this a spiritual conspiracy of the Enemy?

— Do you see how this cripples the effectiveness of the local church? Would anyone really want to cripple Jesus Christ — His body? Do you see the strategic importance of moving from addition by the few to multiplication x multiplication = explosion?

Discussion Takeaways: _____

_____

_____

_____

5. This chapter also has the simple sociogram concept (page 176): List your non-Christian (unchurched) friends, relatives, neighbors, and connections at work or school. Pray for them every day as you look at this sociogram with your name in the middle. This demonstrates that you, not your pastor, not the staff at church, but *you* have the power of relationship influence with these people. Your pastor will never know most of these people (unless God uses YOU to be the conduit of faith in Christ that leads to worship at your church). This is not a program. This is a lifestyle change. It restructures outreach back to the biblical culture Jesus taught. It is what leads to massive growth of the church, called revival.

— Why do you think so many Christians have drifted from God's genius plan of multiplication?

— If you pray for unchurched people in your social network, do you think God might answer your prayers? Why? In the answer to your prayer, what is the likelihood God will use you to bring them to faith?

— Speaking of multiplication, who, and how many people will you invite from your church to be part of a group gathering like this? (1) Make a list. (2) Pray. (3) Act. (4) Multiply. It's not rocket science!

Discussion Takeaways: _____

_____

_____

_____

7 Proven Strategies for Renewal and Revival

Group Gathering Discussion Guide

Week 11: Chapter Ten: Turn Your Service into Dignity
Breakthrough Strategy #6

1. This is the strategy that breaks through *The Ceiling of Identity Theft*. The Bible calls followers of Jesus Ambassadors of Christ (2 Corinthians 5:20). Most Christian churches have downgraded that spiritual calling to the worldly concept of volunteer — a concept that exists nowhere in Scripture — not even close!

Please don't be offended by the heat of my enthusiasm, but this disaster burns me so much I can hardly contain myself. And it's so prevalent, most Christians think volunteerism is practically sacred!

— Do you hear the word "volunteers" around your church? Is it treated like God Himself created the idea without any questions or challenges?

— Have you noticed that a call for "volunteers" is usually a desire to *use* people to complete some job of the institution called church?

— Did it ever occur to you that *God doesn't use people*? He calls people — to join the Ruler of the universe, to be an Ambassador of Christ!

— Do you have jobs around the church to get done? Is that the culture to recruit volunteers?

— Or do you have the children of God around the church, and every one of them is called, including you, to disciple them? These "children" have gifts (not talents), unique gifts given only by the Holy Spirit. Do you help them discover those gifts? Do you help them discover God's calling on their lives?

— When people discuss their gifts and find their calling, they are motivated supernaturally. Is that the culture of your church?

Discussion Takeaways: _____

_____

_____

_____

2. This chapter unearths what sociologists call "intrinsic motivation." Those who work at something *for the fun of it* are significantly more productive than those who work for a paycheck. For intrinsically motivated workers, the paycheck is a bonus. It can even seem like a surprise: "Oh, I get paid to do this?" God's system of supernaturally gifting and calling people to service has been around 2,000 years. (By the way, the word "service" is the secular word for "ministry.") God's work provides intrinsic motivation.

— Do those in your church discover, develop, and use their spiritual gifts?

— Or, do you have volunteers who are used by the church to complete some institutional job?

— Do people consider it the highest privilege to work side by side with the King of the universe, powered supernaturally by the Holy Spirit?

Discussion Takeaways: _____

_____

_____

_____

3. This all begins one of two ways in a church: (1) We have a job to do — let's look for a volunteer. The radically different approach is this: (2) We have a new couple in our church. Do they know their gifts, given by the Holy Spirit? Let's

help them discover their gifts. Then they will have a better idea about the calling God has for them. Then we will help them find the unique ministry that fits God's calling for *them* — even if we have to create one! Then we will find a discipler in that area to disciple them, using the discipling steps. Then *they* will become a discipler of others called to that ministry. Then it will be a movement (not a program)!

> — How does it work in your church? Is the emphasis on the job or the person?
>
> — Can you imagine the untapped power in almost every church?
>
> — What difference would this make for the Kingdom movement?
>
> — Why are there so many churches where these Kingdom principles are buried under corporate programs and volunteerism?

Discussion Takeaways: _____

_____

_____

_____

4. God's plan is that *everyone* is discipled into some ministry. Why? NOT primarily to get something done, but to allow believers to experience the divine fulfillment only experienced by joining hands with the King of the Universe. In this chapter, I wrote about Sunday school teachers.

> — How do you get Sunday school teachers in your church? Do you use pleas from the pastor or Sunday school superintendent? "We (the

organization, institution) need (want to use you) a third grade Sunday school teacher (job of the institution)."

— Or do you greet newcomers, "We want to help you discover your gifts, which direct you to your divine calling"?

— Do Sunday school teachers inherently understand the way God works? Do they pray for and look for, until they find a person with the right spiritual gifts and invite them to be discipled, using the discipleship steps, to become a Sunday school teacher? Do your Sunday school teachers live that approach as part of their calling to multiply?

— When the new Sunday school teachers begin their ministry, is it part of their worldview to be looking for another person to disciple into that ministry, while they do that ministry? Yes.

Discussion Takeaways: _____

_____

_____

_____

5. Another non-biblical concept heard mentioned in many churches is the word "burnout." Even some pastors talk about it. In my book *Burn On or Burn Out*, I write about how Moses went from job to calling. This calling process was both unique and extraordinary. He heard God speak from a burning bush. The bush didn't burn out. It didn't burn up. Why? Because *God was in it*! When God is

in you, in your calling, your ministry, you are on fire. Yet, you don't burn out.

Why? God's fire doesn't burn energy. It produces supernatural energy.

— Do you know someone at church who burned out on ministry? Are
you one of them? (Don't feel bad. I've worked with many pastors.
Even they get burned out.) Is it God's work that burns people out?
Or is it an unbiblical system?

Discussion Takeaways: _____

_____

_____

_____

7 Proven Strategies for Renewal and Revival

Group Gathering Discussion Guide

Week 12: Chapter Eleven: Turn Your Life into Generosity Breakthrough Strategy #7

1. The strategy in this chapter helps you break through *The Ceiling of Recession Impression*. Ever hear some church leader say, "We're short on money"? That is not a biblical concept. It would be more appropriate to say, "We're short on faith," or, "We're short on doing God's work God's way."

This chapter starts with a quote from Jesus in Matthew 6:33: "Seek first his Kingdom and his righteousness, and all these things shall be yours, as well." A famous missionary, Hudson Taylor, said, "God's work, done in God's way, will never lack God's supply."

— Is your church doing God's work?

— Is your church doing God's work God's way?

— Can you know for sure?

— Why do you think Jesus spoke about money so often — even more than He spoke about prayer?

— Do you have an attitude about money that reflects the teaching of Scripture?

— What about your church? Would God approve of the approach to money issues, demonstrated by all those in your church? What do you think?

Discussion Takeaways: _____

_____

_____

_____

2. Generosity is about more than money. Money is our crystallized sweat. It's easy to measure.

— Does your church reflect generosity in service to those in need? Do you?

— Does your church demonstrate generosity in prayer, when Scripture says "pray without ceasing" (1 Thessalonians 5:17)? Do you?

— Does your church practice generosity in hospitality? Are all people (those from the church and guests) genuinely welcomed? Do you live in generous hospitality?

— Most of all, are you generous to God? With your time, use of gifts, service, money?

— Or do you suffer from a poverty mentality, which is foreign to your Creator?

Discussion Takeaways: _____

_____

_____

_____

3. When big decisions face you, do NOT first consider the cost. Focus, first, on this: Is it God's will? Is this what God wants? God pays for what He orders. If it's God's will, it's God's bill, even though you think you have to pay for it. God owns it all.

— Ever hear a proposal from a leader at church that will cost money, and the first thing someone says is something like, "We can't afford that!" Why doesn't someone say, "You're out of order!" The first issue is *always*: Is it God's will? Is it what God wants? How does that work at your church?

— How does that work in your life?

Discussion Takeaways: _____

_____

_____

4. God's will is the key to good decision making. Seeking God's will is always the Kingdom approach to decisions. In the *Healthy Churches Thrive!* spiritual movement, one of several workshops we provide is called *Leading from the Center of God's Will.* It's surprising how revealing this is to most Christians!

　　— Your church will make hundreds of decisions over the next 12 months: some small, some large, perhaps a few that could have significant impact. They are all important. Is your approach to decision making clearly based on what God wants? Is God and what He wants the largest part of the conversation?

　　— What about in your decision making, personally? At work? At home?

　　— How have you developed spiritual decision making with the next generations, your children and their children? Will they function in the Kingdom culture of God's will?

　　— Is generosity an important part of that decision making?

Discussion Takeaways: _____

_____

_____

5. In order to make more decisions, or *any decisions* according to God's will, you will have to know your Bible or seek advice from someone who does. If you are trying to buy a truck, either this year or next year, and you want biblical guidance to make sure you are in God's will for this decision, at this time — you aren't going to find a passage about a truck in the Bible. Kingdom culture is not that simplistic.

However, you can remember the five dimensions of Kingdom culture: (1) Values — what you, as a Christian, consider to be important; (2) Beliefs — what you demonstrate is truth; (3) Attitudes — your posture before God: your stewardship of resources, time, money, work, family; (4) Priorities — what is God calling you to achieve? Would that truck help or hurt the achievement of the priorities God has placed on your life? and (5) Worldviews — how do you see your world and the world of your job, responsibilities, family, church? Does the truck fit those responsibilities?

— Does your church use the resources of outside, objective, trained, biblically committed, knowledgeable experts to guide you in decisions?

— Do you do the same at home?

— Using others to make decisions with help from a biblically committed, knowledgeable expert requires that you recognize a

Kingdom culture issue and a Kingdom character issue. (1) The Kingdom culture issue is your *values*. (2) The Kingdom character issue is *your humility*.

- How does this work in your church?

- How does this work in your life?

Discussion Takeaways: _____

_____

_____

_____

6. This chapter focuses on the Kingdom principle of giving by percentage, NOT a monetary amount. The Bible follows this approach with the "tithe": 10% of what you get goes back to God, off the top. It's about equal sacrifice, not equal giving. It makes sense. However, prior to the Kingdom culture approach of the *Healthy Churches Thrive!* Spiritual Movement, only about 1 in 4 Christians use the percentage, biblical approach to giving (page 214).

— What is your approach?

— What does your church emphasize?

Discussion Takeaways: _____

_____

_____

7 Proven Strategies for Renewal and Revival

Group Gathering Discussion Guide

Week 13: Chapter Twelve: Organic Launch

1. This chapter is focused on "Building the Right Culture the Right Way." The *Healthy Churches Thrive!* Spiritual Movement showcased in *Who Broke My Church?* is not the only approach used today to help churches move toward renewal. However, it is unique because it utilizes a *movement* within your church, not programs.

   Healthy Churches Thrive! is developed as a "bottom-up" approach, not a "top-down" approach. There are two important reasons for this: (1) Jesus used the bottom-up, or organic, approach. (2) It doesn't "blow up" your congregation.

   Program approaches are an easy sell. But when they are finished, the *culture* of the church, the *culture* of the people, has not changed. Programs are not transformational. This is one of the many reasons Jesus did not launch a program. However, many try to reduce Christianity to programs when it comes to seeking meaningful change. Programs are a quick fix. If renewal or revival were quick fixes, the world would have changed long ago. The world of the church would have changed long ago.

Jesus launched an organic movement. It grows from the bottom up. No wonder one of the fruits of the spirit is patience (Galatians 5:22-23). An organic launch is like planting a garden.

— How does your church operate most often? Programs or movement? What has been the result?

— Why do you think a renewal movement is not the first choice for many Christians or churches?

Discussion Takeaways: _____

_____

_____

_____

2. Chapter Twelve says, "*Your patience is the path for organic growth of a healthy church.*" This is like planting a garden.

— Has your church tried programs? Have they changed your church transformationally? Have they changed you transformationally? Are you a *different* person because of a program? (Excluding being burned out.)

— Has your church reached the point where a portion of the people are ready to "dig in" for the long haul and, like the disciples, become patient and willing to grow over time?

— Are you ready?

Discussion Takeaways: _____

_____

_____

_____

3. There are those Christians and churches ready for renewal. In fact, it seems like more Christians are ready every day. Why? Much of secular society has reached bottom. People are eager for meaningful change. They will be the first to lead their churches in a renewal movement. This is not new. It has occurred many times in history. It is exciting to be alive when the Spirit is stirring up holy discontent and spiritual restlessness. This is the first step — and it is entirely the work of God. The next step in this movement is when a core group of people believe it's God's time to respond.

— Do you have a core group of people like that in your church?

— Are you one of them?

Discussion Takeaways: _____

_____

_____

_____

4. The next step, as detailed in Chapter Twelve, is to order an objective assessment of your church. There are several results: (1) to know the extent of holy discontent, (2) to see how many people are now ready to learn about the renewal strength of your church, and (3) to assess the challenges you face — roadblocks to effectiveness. This assessment provides comprehensive recommendations in every area of the life of your church. At Church Doctor Ministries, we call this a "Diagnostic Consultation." It results from your decisions based on (1) your values: is your church important to you, important to God? (2) your character — do you have humility — are you eager to learn all you can?

   — How has the Holy Spirit been working in your church? Do increasing numbers of people sense a stirring that God is ready to move?

   — Is there spiritual leadership in place to guide and direct a journey to spiritual breakthrough?

   — Is there an eagerness — in a core group of people — to grow, to learn, to let God move the church from doing to being, to becoming?

Discussion Takeaways: _____

_____

_____

_____

5. A movement begins like a pebble in a pond. You throw out a pebble and it provides a *small* ring, but the next ring is bigger and the next even bigger (page 230). This is how a movement moves. Eventually there is a tipping point — when the movement can't be humanly stopped. It takes on a life of its own. The tipping point for a church is 40% to 50% of the active people. While God can do anything, this often takes two to three years of continual, intentional spiritual growth in a movement atmosphere. It was three years for the disciples. It takes about the same amount of time for churches today.

    — Are you, personally, ready?

    — Is there a small group in your church that is spiritually ready?

    — If you are not ready, are you willing to wait on the Lord for renewal?

    — If you are ready, are you willing to take the step of faith to move forward, trusting in the Lord?

    Discussion Takeaways: _____

    _____

    _____

6. In the Introduction of *Who Broke My Church?*, I concluded with this thought:

    "If you choose to take this journey, get ready for the greatest God-adventure of

    your life."

    — The answer to discovering whether you are ready is between you

    and God. You, personally, and you, the group.

    — Are you ready?

    — What is God saying to you?

    — What are you going to do about it?

    Discussion Takeaways: _____

    _____

    _____

    _____

Next Steps:

- Learn more: Talk to a representative about *Healthy Churches Thrive!* at

  800-626-8515.

- Pray that God will give you courage to walk the path of a disciple.

It will be the greatest God-adventure of your life.

7 Proven Strategies for
Renewal and Revival

Group Gathering Discussion Guide

Leader's Guide

This section is for the leader of the Gathering Discussion Group that is working through *Who Broke My Church? 7 Proven Strategies for Renewal and Revival* together and coming together 14 times to discuss the book, having read each chapter prior to the gathering. As the leader, the following material will help you prepare for your very important role.

BEFORE YOU EVEN BEGIN: READ THIS SECTION

This *Group Gathering Discussion Guide* is for those who come together to read and discuss the book *Who Broke My Church? 7 Proven Strategies for Renewal and Revival*.

It is very likely that many in the group have never read a book like this or thought about the biblical teaching and life applications of Jesus in this way.

- The reason this book, *Who Broke My Church? 7 Proven Strategies for Renewal and Revival*, is so popular is because it provides a groundbreaking, *refreshed* way to recapture the power and presence of this wonderful, divine organism called the Body of Christ.

- What we call "church" is in deep trouble today. Plateaued, declining, and aging churches are everywhere. Collectively, God's people have lost their influence on society. Civilization, as we know it, is at risk. However, God has a way of renewing those who follow Him — if they're willing.

- Many churches have suffered deeply in effectiveness due to Kingdom drift — wandering in a desert of bylaws and programs, volunteers and fundraisers. We have unintentionally crippled the Body of Christ. But God wants to change that. He is the Great Healer.

- So, from the beginning, as a leader of the group, much of this is going to be very different for you. As the leader, you are NOT going to teach. The principles of the book will guide those in your group toward Jesus' teachings. They are Kingdom principles that are not, as Jesus said, "of this world": not like this world — very different!

- So, <u>you will begin this group differently.</u>

- o You will not advertise in the church bulletin, newsletter, news sheet, or posters.

- o You will not make announcements or beg people to come to this gathering.

- o You are going to practice, as a leader, what it means to lead a <u>movement</u> like Christianity. This movement moves <u>relationally</u>, not institutionally.

- o I know this is different, but, if you want the transformational change the Bible says God wants for His people to experience, you will start this way.

- o What if you are the pastor, and you want to gather the staff or the elders, or leaders of the church for this group? Follow this practice anyway — like a movement. Is it more work? Could you end up with a smaller group? Perhaps! But if you have the faith to practice being a movement leader, you will see more fruit (results). If you don't, you'll get into the book *Who Broke My Church? 7 Proven Strategies for Renewal and Revival* and everyone in the group will realize the right approach anyway! Your choice!

Movement Steps to Start a Group Gathering to Discuss
Who Broke My Church? 7 Proven Strategies for Renewal and Revival

<u>Step #1:</u> Pray now for God to guide you to who He wants in this gathering.

<u>Step #2:</u> Pick the timeframe, location, and other logistics like refreshments.

<u>Step #3:</u> Relationally (face to face), speak to each person/couple/family you believe God is calling into this spiritual experience.

<u>Step #4:</u> Do not ask for an answer right away. Ask them to *pray* about it. Give them a time by which you would like to know. (You are literally practicing what Jesus said, "Come, follow me," a leadership step you will learn about in *Who Broke My Church? 7 Proven Strategies for Renewal and Revival*.) Ask them to ask God to help them make the decision on the basis of: "Is it <u>God's will</u>? Do you feel <u>called</u> to learn more, grow more, be more effective for God's Kingdom at this time?"

<u>Step #5:</u> If they respond, "Yes," tell them they must purchase the book. Unless there is a severe financial issue, they should invest in the price of the book and the *Group Gathering Discussion Guide*.

<u>Step #6</u>: If you want to multiply the movement, as you will learn in *Who Broke My Church? 7 Proven Strategies for Renewal and Revival*, each person will be expected to follow these same steps midway through the experience: to relationally invite others in their social networks and be ready, if God calls them, to lead the next group! (If this occurs and is visible, as the leader, you will disciple the next leader during the last several gatherings of the group, using the six steps of discipling Jesus used, which are explained in the book *Who Broke My Church? 7 Proven Strategies for Renewal and Revival*.)

This is movement thinking, practiced on a smaller scale. You are beginning to benefit by this book before you start reading it! This Kingdom culture changes everything! Why? Because it is the Kingdom culture of Jesus Christ, the Ruler of the universe and the real Head of His Body, the church.

The Use of Different Words

You will notice many words used in this spiritual experience, like "spiritual experience" and "group gathering" instead of "class" or "study." The reason is because this is a movement, not a "study" like a Sunday school class. This is not about learning *more*, but learning *differently*. Movements that renew people use new language. Remember, Jesus said, "New wine needs new wineskins" (Matthew 9:17). "Wineskins" are containers. Words are containers. A renewal movement requires new words.

What is the Goal?

1. The big goal of this experience: Both the book *Who Broke My Church? 7 Proven Strategies for Renewal and Revival* and this *Group Gathering Discussion Guide* are aimed at the transformational *renewal* of Christians in the local church to be well prepared to effectively make disciples for Jesus Christ.

2. Only God can bring the *revival* this world desperately needs — and it is likely coming soon.

3. We can't produce revival — when masses become Christians rapidly.

4. Renewal is about being ready to be used by God to our fullest, as individuals and as churches. It implies personal, spiritual growth.

5. When a large percentage of those in your church (40% - 50%) experience spiritual renewal from reading and personally implementing what you learn from *Who Broke My Church? 7 Proven Strategies for Renewal and Revival* and this growth experience of discussion, God will likely bring what is called an *awakening*.

6. *Knowledge* is a part of Christianity, but not everything. This is a key concept: Spiritual growth is a personal experience.

   - It is not just what you *know*.

   - It is not just what you *do*.

   - It is *who you are* and *who you become*.

7. You are the *leader*, not the teacher.

8. This is not a class, but a *discipleship* group gathering.

9. Those in this group are not students, but *disciples* who want to learn more about following Jesus.

10. This is not merely an intellectual education. It is a *supernatural experience*.

Why is All This So Different?

These are not just different words. Our goal is to get back, closer, to **the Kingdom culture of Jesus**.

Remember how Jesus operated?

1. He *taught*, "The Kingdom of God is like…."

2. However, also, on occasion, he declared, *"The Kingdom of God is not like, not of, this world."*

3. As their leader, Jesus was very *relational* with His followers. So, as the leader of this group, you will be very relational.

   - Be the leader of your group at a relational level.

   - Sit down, guide, direct, no need to dominate.

   - Guide the discussion.

4. Pray often as a group. Ask for prayer requests. *Everyone* take notes of prayer needs. Everyone takes turns praying from those notes, about prayer needs. Anyone can start the group with prayer.

5. If, in the middle of discussion, someone raises a personal need, call for prayer right now. Ask others to lay on hands for prayer, especially those who are nearby the person. This is Kingdom culture from the Scripture.

6. As leader, start each time together by asking, "Anyone want to share what God has been doing in your life since the last time we were together?"

   - If no one starts this, the leader may start this, talking about what God has done in the leader's life.

   - Some people call these stories "testimonies." We recommend you call them "God stories."

7. Jesus taught but also *modeled* ministry.

8. He also *involved* disciples in ministry.

9. As leader, you allow and encourage others to *be in ministry* to others in the group.

10. You also foster *discussion*. You should be more concerned about each person being engaged in the discussion than about getting through the agenda.

What is the Structure of These Group Gatherings?

1. The gathering should last *one hour*. However, if it is feasible, you can go longer.

2. Try to meet in a circle, so eye contact is possible for everyone to see everyone. Do anything necessary to keep it from feeling like a class. The Christian movement is supposed to be relational.

3. Provide food so the atmosphere is more conducive to interaction, a more relaxed setting.

4. Never refer to the group as a class. It is always much more than that.

5. Use touch: handshakes, even hugs if appropriate. The church is family in the Kingdom culture.

6. Use comfortable chairs.

7. Everyone should read one chapter of the book before each gathering of the group (except the first week and the last week). The group gatherings are not for reading the book, but for discussing what has been read. Ask people to come prepared to discuss.

8. Use the discussion guide to encourage discussion, but don't let it become the driving agenda. Ask people what impacted them the most. Ask people what it would look like in your church.

9. If the conversation goes long and you don't finish, don't cut off conversation in the middle. Just take up where you left off last time. The conversation is as important as the content — often more important.

10. There are 12 chapters of *Who Broke My Church?* They include seven proven strategies for renewal and revival.

Your first group gathering should focus on the main points of this leader's guide.

1. The use of different words (above).

2. What is the goal?

3. Why is all this so different?

4. What is the structure of these group gatherings?

5. Also, you should ask (before the first group gathering) those involved to read "Comments from the Author" at the beginning of this *Group Gathering Discussion Guide* and the short Introduction in the book *Who Broke My Church?*

The Leader's Primary Roles

1. To gather the group.

2. To identify the location. You will learn from the book *Who Broke My Church?* that the best place to hold gatherings is often out in the community, not at the church building. This is part of the concept of "turning your church inside out." If it is not possible, find a room at the church that is convenient.

3. Room setup. Make the room look like anything except a classroom — as much as possible. Place the seats in a circle, and the leader should sit anywhere but at the front and never in the same place. The message is: The leader is a facilitator.

4. The primary objectives of the leader include:

   (1) Make sure someone prays at the beginning (not necessarily the leader).

   (2) Spend some time asking if anyone would like to share what God is doing in their life. If no one does, then provide a "God story" yourself, as a leader, about what God has done, if possible.

   (3) Facilitate and encourage discussion to the issues and the focus of each chapter, provided in this guide.

   (4) Gently encourage everyone to be included without forcing anyone.

   (5) Keep anyone from dominating the conversation so that others may be included.

   (6) The discussion is the most important part of this group gathering.

   (7) The leader should listen to the discussion carefully. Wherever possible, summarize the principles of Kingdom culture that are uncovered, which may have been replicated as activities or approaches. Try not to allow the conversation to diminish Kingdom culture into programs and activities. Keep the focus on who we are and who we become, rather than on doing.

   (8) At the end of each session, ask those in the group to pass on what they are learning to others in the church, especially to those with whom they have a relationship, using social media, by phone, or in

person. To do this effectively, encourage each person to keep a small journal or notebook and record takeaway insights.

(9) At the end of each session, ask the question, "How does this change who you are? And how does this change how you will be a different person in the future?"

Another important question to ask at the end is, "What is God saying to you, and what are you going to do about it?"

Structure Summary

Prior to Week #1

1. Read these short items of the Leader's Guide:

   - The use of different words.

   - What is the goal?

   - Why is this so different?

   - What is the structure of these group gatherings?

2. Read the comments from the author, at the beginning of the *Group Gathering Discussion Guide*.

3. Read the short Introduction in *Who Broke My Church? 7 Proven Strategies for Renewal and Revival*.

Prior to Week #2

1. Read Chapter 1 of *Who Broke My Church?* (Do this before the gathering, and write down notes or make underlines in your book and come ready to discuss the issues that are important to you.)

Prior to Week #3

1. Read Chapter 2 of *Who Broke My Church?* (Do this before the gathering, and write down notes or make underlines in your book and come ready to discuss the issues that are important to you.)

Prior to Week #4

1. Read Chapter 3 of *Who Broke My Church?* (Do this before the gathering, and write down notes or make underlines in your book and come ready to discuss the issues that are important to you.)

Prior to Week #5

1. Read Chapter 4 of *Who Broke My Church?* (Do this before the gathering, and write down notes or make underlines in your book and come ready to discuss the issues that are important to you.)

Prior to Week #6 Read Chapter 5 of *Who Broke My Church?* (Do this before the gathering, and write down notes or make underlines in your book and come ready to discuss the issues that are important to you.)

Prior to Week #7

1. Read Chapter 6 of *Who Broke My Church?* (Do this before the gathering, and write down notes or make underlines in your book and come ready to discuss the issues that are important to you.)

Prior to Week #8

1. Read Chapter 7 of *Who Broke My Church?* (Do this before the gathering, and write down notes or make underlines in your book and come ready to discuss the issues that are important to you.)

Prior to Week #9

1. Read Chapter 8 of *Who Broke My Church?* (Do this before the gathering, and write down notes or make underlines in your book and come ready to discuss the issues that are important to you.)

Prior to Week #10

1. Read Chapter 9 of *Who Broke My Church?* (Do this before the gathering, and write down notes or make underlines in your book and come ready to discuss the issues that are important to you.)

Prior to Week #11 Read Chapter 10 of *Who Broke My Church?* (Do this before the gathering, and write down notes or make underlines in your book and come ready to discuss the issues that are important to you.)

Prior to Week #12

1. Read Chapter 11 of *Who Broke My Church?* (Do this before the gathering, and write down notes or make underlines in your book and come ready to discuss the issues that are important to you.)

Prior to Week #13

1. Read Chapter 12 of *Who Broke My Church?* (Do this before the gathering, and write down notes or make underlines in your book and come ready to discuss the issues that are important to you.)

Prior to Week #14

1. Take the Holy Discontent Self-Reflective Tool in the appendix of *Who Broke My Church?* and come ready to discuss.

2. Reflect on the Nine Categories of Spiritual Fruit Before and After Kingdom Culture Strategies in the appendix and come ready to discuss.

3. Consider and be prepared to discuss the next possible steps:

   a. The Diagnostic Analysis and Report for Your Church in the appendix.

   b. The Church-Wide Holy Discontent Analysis for Your Church in the appendix.

4. Complete the Action Plan page in the appendix; this is your personal next steps action.

7 Proven Strategies for Renewal and Revival

Group Gathering Discussion Guide

Appendix

My Personal Action Plan Page

Name: _____

What is God saying to you?

_____
_____
_____
_____
_____
_____
_____

What are you going to do about it?

_____
_____
_____
_____
_____
_____
_____

(continued)

Action Steps

ACTION PLAN	DATE
1.	
2.	
3.	
4.	
5.	
6.	
7.	
8.	
9.	
10.	

The Church-Wide Holy Discontent Analysis for Your Church

1. This is an option for everyone in your church to take the Holy Discontent Survey.

2. It is tabulated by Church Doctor Ministries, and graphics are provided. If your church chooses to enter the *Healthy Churches Thrive!* Spiritual Movement, you will begin with a Diagnostic Consultation.

The Diagnostic Analysis and Report for Your Church

1. Your church can order a full Diagnostic Analysis for your church. It will be based on everyone in the congregation responding to a detailed questionnaire. You will learn the following issues from this Diagnostic Analysis:

    a. Age Distribution

    b. Length of Attendance

    c. Who Became a Christian Before or After Attending Your Church

    d. Leadership Demographics

    e. Top Priorities of Your Church

    f. What Your Church Does Best

    g. Perception of Your Attenders about: The Main Purpose of the Church; The Mission of God; Goal of the Great Commission

    h. Outreach Potential

    i. Spiritual Health and Connectedness

2. An oral report is given to the congregation. Opportunity for Q & A is included.

ABOUT THE AUTHOR

Kent R. Hunter is an author of more than 30 books. He is a consultant to churches, a trainer of pastors, and a discipler of young adults. He launched SEND North America in 2012.

Kent says his reason for being on this earth is to help Christians and churches become more effective for the Great Commission, to make disciples of all peoples. He recognizes that America is the third largest mission field in the world (behind China and India). His passion is to come alongside pastors and church leaders to provide encouragement, direction, and focus, and turn challenges into opportunities for mission through the local church.